The Planner's Navigator

A Practical Guide for Estate Planning for the Florida Resident

Linda Suzzanne Griffin

with assistance from Kit Van Pelt

Introduction

I wrote a book titled *The Survivor's Navigator* in 2013, because of my concern for people dealing with the death of a loved one, I struggled through the death of my father. He was a very young 59 at his death, and I was 33 years old. While I was an attorney and thought I could handle that situation, it was a very difficult time, and I made decisions based on what people told me and suggested. I wanted to help others through that period in their own lives.

In over 30 years of practice helping my clients with their estate planning, I have seen that many people do not understand <u>why</u> they are doing estate planning. If they need estate planning why they can't just "fill out a form" from an office supply store, or off the internet from a legal forms service? After seeing many survivors with their loved ones' "do it yourself" estate planning documents and seeing attorney fees and costs far exceeding the cost to do the estate planning properly, I decided a simple question and answer book, specifically for Florida residents, may help. At the very least, this book will educate individuals in determining whether it is in their best interests to have their estate planning documents prepared by an attorney. My intent is to produce a simple question and answer format which answers various questions about estate planning. If this book gives you guidance, then I have accomplished my goal.

Nothing in this book is intended as legal advice, and nothing contained herein should be interpreted as such. If you are in need of legal advice, then contact your own independent legal counsel. This book is written in light of current (2017) Florida law.

Dedications

I dedicate this book to my clients whose wisdom and hours of enjoyable talks have taught me invaluable lessons over the years. I also dedicate this book to employees of Linda Suzzanne Griffin, P.A., past and present, who have helped me through the years. Finally, I dedicate this book to my husband, Bob Keliher, for his unconditional support and love.

Acknowledgments

I want to thank my father, Harold "Hatch" Griffin, for always believing in me and never telling me there was anything I could not do. He died much too young, but his heart and his integrity live on in me.

I want to thank my grandmother, Corrie Griffin, for sacrificing so much to raise me and for believing in me. She showed me unconditional love.

Thanks also to my mother, Martha Rogers, for being my mother for my first five years and for showing me the unconditional love of a mother.

Thanks to the "mother I never had", Beth Rembert, for always showing me unconditional love and belief in me.

Thanks to my husband, Bob, without whom I would not have found the true joy of living.

To my God and Lord, Jesus Christ, thank you for all the blessings you have given me.

Also I want to thank the following individuals who helped me in the process of creating this book: Kit Van Pelt, Christine Creasey, Heather M. Eady and Laura Kim Hooker.

Table of Contents

Chapter 1: "I Am Too Young"

One late evening during spring break in Clearwater, college students, Joe and Charlie, are walking on the beach. Obviously, as with most college students, their minds are on many other things besides estate planning, assets or medical matters. Unknown to either of them, life is about to change forever. Suddenly, Charlie collapses from what appears to be an alcohol overdose. Joe takes him to the emergency room. Charlie's divorced parents are notified and go directly to the Clearwater hospital. Upon their arrival in Clearwater, they argue about whether to take him back to their home in Ohio or keep him in the Clearwater hospital. While Charlie was being treated, he had to be placed on a ventilator. Charlie did not have a Living Will, Designation of Health Care Surrogate, Durable Power of Attorney or other estate planning documents, and his parents were put in the position to decide what Charlie would want them to do.

Questions:

1. Am I too young to have estate plan documents?

Under Florida law, an individual is an adult at 18, at which time he or she can prepare estate planning documents. Unfortunately, most children will not prepare such documents because they believe it unnecessary, too expensive, and never think about it.

1

Thus, parents should advise and help their children with such documents.

2. What are estate planning documents?

Typically, estate planning documents are your Last Will and Testament, your Durable Power of Attorney, your Designation of Health Care Surrogate, your Living Will and possibly a Revocable Trust. This book will outline these documents in greater detail in later chapters.

3. How do I communicate to my children that they should consider certain documents?

I advise my clients to take advantage of certain family functions or holidays. This is usually is a great time to discuss different issues about the parents' documents as well as the possibility of the children preparing documents. While most young adults do not have the financial means to prepare such documents, many parents are willing to pay for those documents.

4. Did Charlie really need to have a Living Will?

A Living Will is an advanced directive to determine a person's desires as they relate to terminal illness. You have to look no further than the Terri Schiavo case to understand how a young person can lapse into a coma or remain on a respirator with no hope of recovery. If there is no Living Will, then litigation can arise between family members who disagree on the individual's desire in such a situation. Charlie's parents are already arguing about where Charlie is to be in the hospital. Imagine the tougher decision to take him off the ventilator!

5. What happens if Charlie's parents disagree as to whether to take Charlie off of the ventilator?

Of course the next stop is the court house which can be very expensive and time consuming. By the time a decision is rendered, the medical bills, attorney fees and costs can bankrupt a family.

6. Why would a young adult ever need a Last Will and Testament if they have no assets?

I frequently hear this question because people think estate planning is only for rich people. If you are young and you are employed or even still in college, you may have some life insurance or assets given to you by relatives, or you might be participating in a 401k plan, an individual retirement plan ("IRA") or some such retirement vehicle through your employer. Upon your death, those assets are distributed accordingly to your beneficiary designation or a Last Will and Testament which directs where those assets are to be distributed. Many young people think they do not have any assets; however, if they look closely and see what assets they really do have, then it is advisable to have documents to provide where the assets are to be distributed.

7. Can the Living Will, Durable Power of Attorney or Designation of Health Care Surrogate direct who will handle these decisions?

Absolutely. Such documents will name someone to make those decisions for you. The Living Will directs what decisions you would want the person to make if you are terminally ill. The Durable Power of Attorney and Designation of Health Care Surrogate let the individuals make decisions on your behalf should you become incapacitated. If Charlie had a Living Will, then Charlie's wishes would control rather than his parents' decision.

Chapter 2: Designation of Health Care Surrogate

Sally and her daughter, Amy, are meeting at Starbucks and having a conversation about Sally's other daughter (and Amy's sister), Marie. Sally chokes on a piece of food and unfortunately ends up in the emergency room at the local hospital. She does not have any documents as to who can make health decisions for her, and, unfortunately, her husband has passed away. Sally's two daughters do not get along, and they are both advising the physicians (in a conflicting manner) what should be done for her care. The Designation of Health Care Surrogate can prevent such a situation.

Questions:

1. What is a Designation of Health Care Surrogate?

It is a document naming another person (a "surrogate") as your representative to make medical decisions for you if you are unable to make them yourself. You can include instructions about any treatment you want or do not want, similar to a Living Will. You can also designate alternate surrogates.

2. Who can be the surrogate?

Any adult who is not incapacitated can act as a surrogate. You will want to designate a person whom you trust implicitly to comply with what you have identified as the medical treatments, procedures, etc., you do, or do not, want the surrogate to authorize on your behalf. Sally may decide that Amy is better at making health care decisions and Marie is better at making financial decisions.

3. What kind of decisions can a surrogate make?

Such decisions can include providing informed consent on medical decisions, authorizing transfer and admission to or from a health care facility, employing and discharging health care personnel, providing for home care and companionship, giving or withholding consent to any medical procedure, test or treatment, including surgery and the administration of pain-relieving drugs, executing documents regarding your care and many other relevant decisions. You should discuss this with your intended surrogate and identify the parameters of what you want the intended surrogate to do for you. The surrogate has, in essence, the same rights to request or refuse treatment that you would have if capable of making and communicating decisions.

4. What if there are two named surrogates because the parent does not want to hurt either child's feelings?

Good intentions go out the window when it comes to naming two children who may not agree on anything to act as co-surrogates. The best practice is to name one as primary and the second as alternate. If Amy and Marie are named and they do not agree, then litigation may ensue, costing even more in legal fees, time and delay.

5. How do you sign the Designation of Health Care Surrogate?

The written document designating a surrogate to make health care decisions for you is signed by you in the presence of two subscribing adult witnesses. If you are unable to sign the instrument, you may, in the presence of witnesses, direct that another person sign your name as required therein. An exact copy of the instrument shall be provided to your surrogate.

The person designated as your surrogate can not act as witness to the execution of the Designation of Health Care Surrogate. At least one person who acts as a witness cannot be your spouse or a blood relative.

6. Will a hospital honor the Designation of Health Care Surrogate?

Preparation of your Designation of Health Care Surrogate by a Florida attorney, with proper signatures and witnesses, should ensure that document is honored by most health care providers. If you are unsure whether or not a hospital or health care provider will honor your Designation of Health Care Surrogate, ask to meet with the provider's or hospital's personnel in advance of an appointment or hospital admission.

7. As I understand, new legislation was passed in 2015. How does that affect this document?

Under prior 2015 law, the Designation of Health Care Surrogate became effective only when you become incapable of making and communicating your own health care decisions.

In recent Florida legislation, you now have the option of authorizing your surrogate to receive medical information while you are still capable of making decisions. Further, you can also authorize your surrogate to make medical decisions for you if you are not incapacitated. However, any medical decisions you make, either verbally or in writing, while possessing capacity, shall supersede any medical decisions made by your surrogate.

Chapter 3: Living Will

Amanda and Charlie have been married for quite a long time and have three adult children, Amy, Sue and Cliff. Amanda and Charlie, unfortunately, have each struggled with progressing dementia and were each recently diagnosed with a terminal illness. Both are on life support in the same hospital. As you can imagine, there is much consternation and disagreement among the children as to what to do. Amanda and Charlie do not have Living Wills, and their children have no idea as to what their parents' wishes are regarding the decisions that must be made in dealing with their present medical circumstances. Needless to say, all three children are losing sleep, and arguments and dysfunctional activities are becoming the norm. This chapter will discuss what a Living Will is and how it can help you.

Questions:

1. What is a Living Will?

A Living Will is a written statement of the kind of medical care you want or do not want **should you have a terminal condition**. Its purpose is to direct the withholding or withdrawal of life prolonging procedures.

2. What is the difference between a Living Will and a Last Will and Testament and a Do Not Resuscitate Form ("DNR")?

A Living Will is a declaration of medical care if you have a terminal condition.

A Last Will and Testament is the document by which your assets are distributed after your death.

A DNR is written by a doctor and instructs medical professionals to not perform CPR if you stop breathing or your heart stops beating. You do not need a terminal condition to use a DNR. Unlike a Living Will, a DNR is specific to CPR and will not give medical professionals instructions for any other medical treatment you would or would not want performed.

3. Are there different definitions of terminal illness?

A terminal condition is defined as "... a condition caused by injury, disease, or illness from which there is no reasonable medical probability of recovery and which, without treatment, can be expected to cause death."

4. Can I make my own decision if I still have the capacity to do so?

Certainly, the Living Will only addresses situations where you are no longer able to make those decisions on your own.

5. Is there a writing or signature formality?

You must sign the Living Will in the presence of a notary and two witnesses. A witness cannot be your spouse or a blood relative. If you are unable to physically sign, one of the witnesses can sign for you in your presence and under your direction.

6. Can I receive CPR or other life prolonging procedures if I am terminal?

Your individual Living Will specifies what medical care you do and do not authorize if you are declared to be in a terminal state/condition.

7. What other kind of issues can be addressed by a Living Will?

Supplemental to instructions regarding your (terminal) medical care, your Living Will can also include provisions for giving you food and water, CPR, dialysis, medications, engaging hospice care and others.

8. Are there different Living Wills for different religions?

A Living Will can be customized to take into consideration your religious views and positions concerning end-of-life issues. Several religions, including Jehovah's Witnesses, Southern Baptists, Judaism, Catholicism and others, currently have their own websites that deal directly with this issue.

Chapter 4: Durable Power of Attorney

After paying off their mortgage, Edith and George went to their safe deposit box to obtain a copy of their house deed. The deed indicates that their house is held in joint names. Unfortunately, on their way home they are in a terrible car crash, leaving George incapacitated from his injuries and a resulting stroke. Edith and George had gone to the bank to get their deed because they planned on selling their house and were moving to a condo on the beach. A closing date had been scheduled but closing documents had not yet been prepared. The title company and their attorney tell Edith that if she has a Power of Attorney ("POA") for George, she can sign the documents for him. Further, if she has a <u>Durable</u> Power of Attorney ("DPOA"), she can sign the documents and the DPOA is effective whether or not he regains capacity prior to the closing. Edith has come to my office and asks these questions because she does not understand the POA. She has a document that was prepared in Texas that is titled "Durable Power of Attorney" and wants to know whether it is effective in Florida.

Questions:

1. What exactly does a DPOA provide?

By signing a DPOA, you have named someone (an "agent") to handle specifically enumerated financial decisions in a manner that you direct, even if you become incapacitated. Thus, the Power of Attorney is "durable."

2. What is the difference between a POA and a DPOA?

A POA is a legal document delegating authority from you to your agent, someone whom you trust and know will act on your behalf in accordance with your wishes. A POA is usually signed for a particular transaction, such as a closing on a house. The POA <u>terminates</u> should you become incapacitated, die or the purpose for the POA is completed.

A DPOA remains effective (is "durable") even if you become incapacitated, and, like the POA, terminates at your death.

3. What powers can be put in a POA?

The powers granted by your POA can be limited or broad, and your agent can perform the acts the POA allows. Generally, a POA is limited to specific transactions. For example, George may have given Edith a POA to sign the closing documents at the closing. If, however, George is incapacitated, the POA is ineffective because the POA terminates at George's incapacity. Thus, the need for a DPOA is created.

4. Has Florida law changed its requirements for a DPOA?

Yes, in 2011, Florida law changed dramatically regarding DPOAs to better define the powers you authorize your agent to use. In the past, agents were taking advantage of the DPOA. The person giving rights to their agent did not understand the extent of the powers that an agent could use. Now the law requires you to specifically initial certain "superpowers" so you understand what powers you are giving to your agent. This initially should eliminate confusion for you, your agent and the person or institution involved with assisting your agent to act on your behalf.

5. What are the signature requirements for a DPOA?

Your DPOA must be signed by you and two witnesses and a notary must acknowledge your signature for the DPOA to be valid under Florida law.

6. What are some powers that can be placed in the DPOA?

Your DPOA depends on your specific needs. For example, it might be used to allow access to bank accounts, sign contracts, handle financial transactions, manage financial investments, apply for government benefits, make charitable contributions or complete charitable pledges, sign legal documents for you or even create trusts and make gifts.

7. What are examples of the "super powers" that have to be specifically provided for in the DPOA and be initialed?

You must specifically authorize, via initialing or otherwise by specific affirmation or rejection, powers related to income tax returns, investments, retirement plans, charitable pledges, transfers to trusts, gifts, 529 Plans, charitable gifts, government benefits, disclaimers and insurance and annuities.

8. What powers could be put in a DPOA that might not be a common situation?

Some powers that you may want to consider are making gifts in accordance with your estate plan, to plan for estate or gift tax situations, retirement benefit planning and beneficiary designations.

9. Is the DPOA effective as soon as you sign it?

Yes. Florida discontinued the "springing" DPOA when the law changed in 2011 and now becomes effective immediately.

10. How do you define incapacity for purposes of "triggering the use" of the DPOA?

You and your attorney will decide, in advance, what situations need to happen prior to the release of any documents relating to your incapacity, including your DPOA. For example, you may want to have the document(s) released only upon your own instructions, oral or written; you may require that one medically licensed doctor provide a written opinion as to your condition; or you may require evidence that you have disappeared, are absent or are being detained under duress, all of which make you unable to act in your own best interests.

11. How do you protect yourself from having the agent use your DPOA while you are still capable of making your own decisions?

You may hold the DPOA document until such time as you feel you need help and then give it to the agent. You may also leave the DPOA with the attorney who prepared the DPOA, asking the attorney to deliver it to your agent under certain specific conditions, which you set forth with the attorney at the time of signing.

If you are concerned about unauthorized use of your DPOA, think carefully about what powers you want your agent to have. Several options are available to you to create limited authority or limited circumstance DPOAs, making sure that the DPOA will give your agent only certain powers and nothing more.

12. Who should I appoint as agent of my DPOA?

Ideally, you should name as your agent, a relative or friend whom you trust, to handle specific legal and financial responsibilities in accordance with your wishes. It is always a good idea to ask the person whether he or she is willing to take on the responsibility you wish to give. If not, plan to name someone else.

13. How do I revoke a DPOA once it has been given to my agent?

A DPOA may be revoked by expressing the revocation in a subsequently executed DPOA or other writing signed by the principal.

Once the DPOA has been given to an agent, the best practice, even if the agent gives you back the copy or original, is to go to each of your financial institutions and provide them with a new DPOA which clearly states "I revoke all prior Durable Powers of Attorney".

14. What if I do not have a DPOA?

If you do not have a DPOA and something happens to you that makes it impossible for you to take care of your daily finances, then your family or physician may be forced to petition the court for appointment of a legal guardian.

15. How does a DPOA avoid a guardianship?

Because the DPOA can authorize an agent to transfer property, borrow money, handle bank accounts and pay bills, it easily avoids the need to have a guardian appointed by the court to undertake these tasks, thereby saving the family (or person) unnecessary expense and time. If Edith did not have a DPOA signed by George, then she cannot sign for George, possibly necessitating a guardianship for the simple task of signing a deed!

16. What exactly is a guardianship and do I need an attorney for a guardianship?

A guardianship is a legal process whereby a person with a debilitating physical and/or mental condition is declared incapacitated, and a guardian of the person and property is appointed by the court. The process is usually quite expensive, with required court appearances and testimony by experts, ongoing court supervision and regular accountings.

17. Will my DPOA in Texas work in Florida?

If your Texas DPOA was properly executed under Texas law, then it may be used in Florida, BUT its use will be subject to Florida's Power of Attorney Act and other state laws. The agent may act only as authorized by Florida law and the terms of the DPOA. Further, even though the DPOA may be valid, an institution may require an affidavit by an attorney stating the DPOA is valid, which creates more expense and delay. If a person moves to Florida, then the better practice is to obtain a Florida DPOA prepared by a licensed Florida attorney.

Chapter 5: Last Will and Testament

Sam and Sally have been married for 10 years and have a minor daughter, Suzie. Sam and Sally do not have a lot of assets, but Sam has his work income, a life insurance policy and a retirement plan. Together, he and Sally own their home with a mortgage owed to the bank. Sam and Sally, like many young couples, do not understand a Last Will and Testament or if they even need one because they have designated their spouse as the primary beneficiary of their 401(k) plans, life insurance policies with Suzie as the contingent beneficiary. Their home is titled in joint names. If anything happens to both of them, all of their assets would be distributed to Suzie. So, isn't that enough? Why would they need a Last Will and Testament?

Questions:

1. What is a Last Will and Testament?

A Last Will and Testament describes how your property is distributed upon your death. It must be in writing, signed by you, and properly witnessed by two persons. A Last Will and Testament should also be self-proving to avoid having to find witnesses upon death. A self-proof is an affidavit stating that the testator(he)/testatrix(her) signed the Last Will and Testament and that the witnesses and the testator/testatrix signed the Last Will and Testament in the presence of each other.

A Last Will and Testament may contain:

- ❖ Specific distributions of property or cash

- ❖ Provision for a separate writing for personal items

- ❖ Trust provisions to control how the property is to be distributed after your death

- ❖ Name of a guardian for your minor children

- ❖ Name of a personal representative to handle payment of bills and coordination and distribution of your estate

- ❖ Powers of the personal representative

2. How does a life insurance policy, 401(k) or individual retirement account ("IRA") pay to a beneficiary?

In most instances, your life insurance policy will be paid to your named beneficiary(ies) upon receipt by the life insurance company of an original death certificate.

Payout to the beneficiary(ies) of your 401(k) or IRA will require your beneficiary(ies) to complete the plan's claim form documents. Because tax consequences come into play with a 401(k) payout, the Internal Revenue Service (the "IRS") offers options for plans regarding the payout choices to your beneficiaries. The payout terms of the plan and the beneficiary's(ies') relationship to you will affect their individual tax liability. Because Suzie is a minor, depending on the amount in the 401(k) plan, a guardianship for Suzie may have to be established to receive the 401(k) benefits.

3. What is a pay on death ("POD") account?

Many banks and/or brokerage accounts allow POD or transfer on death ("TOD") accounts. This allows, much like life insurance beneficiary designations, the account to be payable directly to a named individual. This, however, creates issues when the named individual is a minor, such as in Suzie's case.

4. Is a Last Will and Testament necessary if there are beneficiary designations on all accounts and POD or TOD accounts?

Yes, a Last Will and Testament should always be drafted, especially if you have minor children, own a business or are self-employed, just to name a few reasons. Although the laws governing intestacy (death without a will) protect your family, the ability to specifically designate how you want certain personal situations to be addressed, including distributions from your estate, is lost. Further, Sam and Sally could provide for Suzie and avoid a guardianship of the property.

5. Who can be the personal representative under a Last Will and Testament and what is a personal representative?

A personal representative is an individual or entity named in a Last Will and Testament or by Florida law to handle the probate of assets. You can name a person over 18 years old, who is a Florida resident, has never have been convicted of a felony and is mentally and physically able to perform the duties as a personal representative. A nonresident can qualify as a personal representative only if that person is a blood relative of the decedent, a legally adopted child or adoptive parent of the decedent, or the spouse of a blood relative. If you do not want to name an individual as your personal representative, you can name a professional such as your attorney or CPA, a nationally chartered financial institution or Florida chartered institution such as a bank or trust company.

6. What are the responsibilities of a personal representative?

Under Florida law, a personal representative is responsible to observe the same standards of care in the administration of a probate estate that are applicable to trustees. The personal representative has a duty to settle and distribute the decedent's estate in accordance with the terms of your Last Will and Testament, Florida law, and in the best interests of the estate and any interested persons, including creditors.

The most important duties of a Florida personal representative are as follows:

❖ Locate your Last Will and Testament

❖ Confer with the lawyer who will serve as attorney for your estate and arrange with the lawyer for probate of your Last Will and Testament

❖ Talk with family members to determine their immediate financial needs

❖ Make tentative arrangements for support and maintenance payments to be paid to your loved ones during the settlement period

❖ Seek court authority to serve as your personal representative

❖ Manage your property, including your business, during the settlement period

❖ Distribute your property according to the directions in your Last Will and Testament

❖ File your final personal income tax return

❖ Choose a tax year for your estate

❖ File your estate's federal income tax returns

❖ File any state income and death tax returns

❖ Complete and file the federal estate tax return

❖ Become a party to litigation, if any, relating to the estate

❖ Sell assets, such as real estate, stocks and bonds

❖ Invest assets that are not needed immediately for distribution or expenses

❖ Account to the beneficiaries for all actions taken during administration

7. Does a Last Will and Testament avoid probate? What exactly is probate?

No, a Last Will and Testament does not avoid probate.

Probate is a legal process through which the assets of a deceased person are properly distributed to the heirs or beneficiaries under a Last Will and Testament, or if there is no Last Will and Testament, according to Florida law. Probate specifically applies to decedent's assets which are titled in the decedent's name alone that do <u>not</u> have named primary or contingent beneficiary designations.

8. How can I avoid probate?

There are several avenues available for positioning your assets so a probate is not necessary.

The most common of these is to create a Revocable Living (or Inter Vivos) Trust (discussed in Chapter 6), which may alleviate the issues associated with joint ownership and beneficiary designations.

Another method commonly used to keep assets from the probate process is to name a beneficiary on your individually owned bank and investment accounts. Using the TOD or POD designation on your bank account allows you to name a beneficiary who will own the asset upon your death. If you have investment accounts and use the TOD or POD designations, then, at your death, probate is avoided because the asset is distributed directly to the named beneficiary, the step-up in basis for income tax purposes is preserved, and claims of the named beneficiary's creditors cannot reach those assets while you are alive.

If the property is titled jointly with right of survivorship, the probate process is also avoided until there are no more surviving joint owners. The property is then subject to probate. In the situation where your gross estate is in excess of the available applicable exclusion amount for federal estate tax purposes, the use of jointly-owned property may cause federal estate tax issues. Joint assets may also create asset protection issues as discussed in Chapter 9 and Chapter 12. The use of joint property may be the least advantageous way to avoid probate.

9. What provisions can be put in a Last Will and Testament other than the disposition of assets?

Several other provisions your Last Will and Testament can address include, but are not limited to, allocation of taxes, expenses and debts, specific duties you wish the personal representative to address, the creation of individual trusts and provisions for the guardianship of your minor children.

10. What is the difference between a guardianship of the person and a guardianship of the property of my minor children?

The guardian of the person is a person appointed by the court to make decisions regarding support, care, education, health and welfare of a minor (or incapacitated adult). The guardian of the property is a person appointed by the court to administer the property of a minor (or incapacitated adult).

11. What if I want a specific person to be a guardian of the person for my minor child?

You can name this person in your Last Will and Testament. You should choose someone you trust and add a clause to your Last Will and Testament that you want that person to raise your children if you die. In your Last Will and Testament, name one person as guardian and one person as an alternate (in case the first one cannot fulfill the position) for EACH of your children. You can choose a different guardian for each child. If, however, you desire that your children be raised together, put that in your document.

You can also prepare a Designation of Preneed Guardian document which lists your preference of appointment of a guardian, should a guardianship become necessary. This document can be filed with the court.

12. What if Sam and Sally get divorced and both are fit to act as guardian of the person of Suzie, but Sally does not want Sam to be such guardian?

Sam and Sally should each name a guardian for each child in his or her own Last Will and Testament, regardless of the parents' financial resources.

Unfortunately, even if Sally names another person and Sally dies first, and Sam is competent and not "unfit", then Sam will, more likely than not, be named guardian of the person of Suzie. Nevertheless, it is important that Sally name her preferences if Sam cannot act, or if he is determined "unfit" to handle the guardianship. Sally can always provide in a trust for financial matters to be handled by someone other than Sam, thus avoiding a guardianship of the property.

13. What happens if my minor child inherits any assets?

In Florida, if a child under the age of 18 inherits any asset having a value greater than $15,000, then a court-mandated guardianship for the property of the minor is necessary. Homestead is a more complicated issue and is discussed in Chapter 11.

14. Can Sally create a provision in her Last Will and Testament in which Suzie will not receive money until she is 25 years old?

Of course. You can include a section, referred to as a testamentary or "shallow" trust, in which you designate a trustee until the child reaches a certain age, protecting the assets. During such period of time the trustee has the power to distribute income and principal to the child as you direct in the "shallow trust" of your Last Will and Testament.

15. Can Sally change her Last Will and Testament before she dies?

Certainly. If Sally only has minor changes or additions to her Last Will and Testament, her attorney can prepare a document called a Codicil to deal with those issues. However, if Sally wants to make significant changes, it is best to have a new Last Will and Testament prepared and signed.

16. Does a Last Will and Testament help me avoid taxes?

Not necessarily. However, several estate tax planning options are available to you, specifically Irrevocable Trusts, which can reduce your taxable estate (not your probate estate) and may permit you to both retain your assets and benefit from them. Taxes are discussed further in Chapter 7.

Chapter 6: The Revocable Trust

Molly and Jerry have been married for 40 years and have three children, Adam, Bentley and Carol, all of whom are in their mid to late thirties. Over the course of their marriage, Jerry and Molly have accumulated approximately three million dollars between them. Their children are generally doing well. However, Bentley seems to be struggling with a drug and alcohol problem and periodically goes "on and off the wagon".

They want to give their children equal shares of their assets, but because of Bentley's problems, they are reconsidering their options as they do not want funds to be available for drugs and/or alcohol. While Adam and Carol are doing well, Molly and Jerry do not want to treat any child differently in fear of hurt feelings.

They have heard about a Revocable Trust, but do not understand how one works or how it could help their situation. They also do not understand why someone would want to create a Revocable Trust if a Last Will and Testament would suffice. They currently have Last Wills and Testaments, however, these documents do not address the issue of Bentley.

Molly and Jerry have retained an estate planning attorney to discuss the advantages of a Last Will and Testament and a Revocable Trust and also to explain how each of these documents would affect them.

Questions:

1. How does a Last Will and Testament differ from a Revocable Trust?

A Last Will and Testament is a document describing how property you own individually (or assets with no beneficiary designation or a TOD or POD beneficiary designation) is to be distributed upon your death, and names a personal representative, as the person (or entity) to gather your assets, distribute them and ensure that all expenses and creditor's claims associated with your probate estate are properly administered. A Last Will and Testament is administered through a probate process with the court.

Alternatively, if you title your property in the name of a Revocable Trust during your lifetime, such property is generally not subject to a probate process. A Revocable Trust also provides greater flexibility regarding when and how your trust assets are distributed to your beneficiaries. Further, a Last Will and Testament is deposited with the probate court and is a public record while a Revocable Trust generally is not filed with the court.

2. What is a Revocable Trust and what does "Revocable" mean?

A Revocable Trust is a trust, as evidenced by a trust document, that is created by an individual during his or her lifetime. "Revocable" means that the trust creator (grantor or settlor) has the ability to change his or her mind regarding the trust, either in part or completely, while living. The grantor can "revoke" the trust, amend the trust or restate the trust as the grantor wishes.

3. Does Revocable Trust mean that there is absolutely no probate process and no court supervision?

Not necessarily. Assets properly titled in the name of your Revocable Trust do not (generally) have to proceed through a probate process. Any assets not titled in the name of your Revocable Trust but titled in your individual name or <u>without</u> a beneficiary designation, are generally con-sidered probate assets and subject to probate court supervision.

4. If assets are in a Revocable Trust, are any expenses incurred for the administration of a Revocable Trust similar to probate?

The trustee of a Revocable Trust has duties for which the trustee can charge a fee during administration of the trust. The trustee must maintain the assets, prepare statements of account and tax reports to the trust beneficiaries, make appropriate distributions, file and pay taxes and perform other administrative tasks. The attorney for the trustee is also entitled to attorney fees. The trustee may also incur expenses for hiring other professionals such as a certified public accountant or an investment advisor.

5. How do I know if assets are titled in the name of my Revocable Trust so as to avoid the probate process?

You must physically re-title your assets during your lifetime to ensure that they are part of your Revocable Trust upon your death. Generally bank or brokerage statements will state your name, as Trustee or u/a/d (under agreement dated), etc.

6. Could Molly or Jerry place provisions in their Revocable Trust to address Bentley's situation?

Yes, they have the ability to draft special terms within their Revocable Trusts for each beneficiary's situation.

7. What happens if Bentley does go "off the wagon?" Can provisions be made in the

Revocable Trust preventing him from getting monies?

In Bentley's situation, several separate options are available to you, including but not limited to, establishing a separate "trust" within your Revocable Trust and providing for substance abuse provisions requiring the trustee to withhold monies if drug testing results confirm suspected drug use.

8. Who can be the trustee of my Revocable Trust?

Generally, during your lifetime, unless you are incapacitated, you can and should be the trustee. Your Revocable Trust can state who will act as successor trustee(s) should you become incapacitated and after your death. Any individual over age eighteen (18) who is not incapacitated can act as trustee. Examples of individuals who can act as trustee are family members, friends, CPA's, attorneys, financial advisors, etc. Corporations, such as banks and trust companies, can act as trustee if they are licensed to act in Florida.

9. What is an incentive trust?

An incentive trust is a trust designed to encourage or discourage certain behaviors by using distributions of trust income or principal as an incentive. A typical incentive trust might encourage a beneficiary to complete a degree, enter a profession, or abstain from harmful conduct such as substance abuse.

10. Can I provide in a Revocable Trust that, if a child dies before me, their share is distributed to their children?

Certainly. By associating the term "per stirpes" with each child's (or all children's) names in your Revocable Trust document, you will be designating their heirs.

11. Is a Revocable Trust generally more expensive to prepare than a Last Will and Testament?

As a Revocable Trust can be significantly more comprehensive than a Last Will and Testament, the cost will probably be greater.

12. If I have a Revocable Trust, then do I need a Last Will and Testament?

Yes.   You will need a "pour-over" Last Will and Testament, directing distributions of your assets from your probate estate to your Revocable Trust. Ideally, your assets should be properly titled in the name of the Revocable Trust prior to your death. Unfortunately, experience demonstrates that this retitling process is not often done. Further, retitling may not be appropriate for all assets such as homestead (see Chapter 11).

13. How do you retitle assets in the name of a Revocable Trust?

How you retitle the asset depends on the type of asset. You can retitle by (a) advising a bank or brokerage company and/or financial advisor to retitle the asset(s); (b) preparing a deed to transfer real estate into the trust; (c) preparing a transfer and assignment for tangible personal property or the like; (d) preparing a new stock certificate, LLC membership interest or partnership interest; (e) preparing new beneficiary designation forms.

14. Retitling sounds complicated. Do I need to do this myself or can my attorney or financial advisor help me?

Retitling assets can become very time consuming and frustrating. Attorneys can help you, but generally for a fee. Your financial advisor may or may not charge a fee. It is critical that, at the signing of your Revocable Trust, you discuss with your attorney which assets need to be retitled and whom will assist you in the process.

15. What kind of provisions can I have in the Revocable Trust besides the provisions for my children and does it matter what I include in the Revocable Trust?

Your Revocable Trust may include provisions such as the care of your pet(s), substance abuse issues, special needs situations, ages at which time a child or grandchild receives their distributions, powers, duties, provisions for nominations of successor trustees, etc. And, yes, it DOES matter what you include in your Revocable Trust, because the trustee needs guidance as to how to administer the Revocable Trust with accuracy as to your intended wishes.

Chapter 7: Estate Tax and Estate Income Taxes

Jerry and Molly understand estate taxes and how they work. They want to make sure no estate taxes are due upon either of their deaths. They want to explore the options available to them to help them understand what kind of deductions they can take to save estate taxes in the future if the value of their estate exceeds the applicable exclusion amount.

Questions:

1. Exactly what is an estate tax?

If you are a United States citizen and/or resident, the federal government imposes an estate tax on all assets owned by you at your death, whether in probate or your Revocable Trust. The Internal Revenue Code defines what is includable and deductible. This tax is a "one-time" tax incurred for the "privilege" of transferring your property.

2. What is the applicable exclusion amount?

A United States citizen it entitled to an applicable exclusion amount ($5,490,000 in 2017) increased each year by an inflation factor. The total of lifetime gifts and assets transferred at death exceeding the applicable exclusion amount are taxed at 40% (rate in 2017).

3. How can a deduction reduce the amount of estate taxes?

Valid deductions reduce the size of your federal taxable estate. Such deductions include, but are not limited to, distributions to spouses qualifying for the marital deduction, payments for creditors, funeral expenses, distributions to charities qualifying for the charitable deduction, attorney fees, accounting fees, trustee fees and personal representative fees.

4. What kind of charitable gifting can I make and can charitable gifts be used in my estate plan to save estate taxes?

You can make charitable gifts either during your lifetime or at your death pursuant to your Last Will and Testament or your Revocable Trust. One option is a Charitable Remainder Trust ("CRT") whereby you or someone you designate would receive lifetime distributions (calculated according to IRS tables) and upon your or your designee's death, the balance remaining in the trust would be distributed to the charity(ies) of your choice. The amount distributed to the charity(ies) would be a deduction either on your income tax return (if made during life) or your taxable estate if made at death.

5. Can I make a charitable gift during my lifetime and still use the assets?

Yes. As described in #4 above, a form of CRT would allow you use of your assets during your lifetime.

6. What is the difference between a CRT and a Charitable Lead Trust ("CLT")?

The major difference between a CRT and a CLT is when the charity receives the benefit. As mentioned in #4 above, in a CRT, you (or your designated beneficiary) receive lifetime income, with any remaining principal going to the charity at your death. The opposite situation occurs with a CLT. The charity receives income initially, under specific terms, and at the end of the trust term, the remaining funds are distributed to your named beneficiaries.

7. I've heard of a pooled income fund. What does that do?

If you do not have sufficient assets to set up an individual charitable trust or want to make smaller contributions over a period of time, then you can contribute to a jointly-owned fund and "pool" your interest. An income tax deduction is available in the year your contribution is made and income is paid until the last income beneficiary in the "pool" dies, at which time the remaining interest is transferred to the charity.

8. What is a gift annuity?

A gift annuity involves making a direct gift to a charity and designating a beneficiary (person) to receive the income from that gift during his or her lifetime. This arrangement is beneficial to both the charity and the beneficiary, and upon the death of the beneficiary, the charity retains any remaining principal and undistributed income.

9. What other assets can I give to a charity to reduce my gift and estate taxes?

You can "give" a charity all or a portion of a home or other real property while you are alive, and retain a life estate in the real estate until you die. Upon your death, the property will then go to the charity, and a tax deduction is received by your estate for the value of the property passing to the charity. Further, the property is removed from your taxable estate for estate tax purposes.

You can also donate a life insurance policy or retirement benefits, either existing or new, to a charity by making the charity both the owner and the beneficiary, resulting in yet another income tax deduction for the contribution.

10. What other kind of planning can be done to save estate taxes prior to our death?

Some of the planning techniques are as follows: (1) grantor-retained annuity trust ("GRAT"); (2) sale to an intentionally-defective trust; (3) gifting to a limited liability company or family limited partnership to use discounts; (4) qualified personal residence trust ("QPRT"); (5) irrevocable gifting trust; (6) dynasty trust; and (7) irrevocable life insurance trust ("ILIT").

The above techniques, including the GRAT, QPRT and ILIT are complicated and need technical legal and tax advice to pursue.

11. I have heard about portability. What is it and how do I use it?

Portability was passed in the 2010 Tax Act and made permanent in 2013. The surviving spouse can use the predeceased spouse's unused applicable exclusion amount if the surviving spouse files a federal estate tax return for the predeceased spouse even if the estate is not otherwise taxable.

Thus, assume Molly dies in 2017 and has used none of her applicable exclusion amount. Jerry then files an estate tax return for Molly within nine (9) months from the date of her death (or fifteen (15) months if an extension is filed) and elects portability. Jerry will not only have his own applicable exclusion amount ($5.490 million in 2017), but he can also use Molly's unused applicable estate tax exclusion amount of $5.490 million for a total of $10.98 million. Special drafting in your Last Will and Testament and Revocable Trust should address portability.

12. What is the estate or trust INCOME tax return?

IRS Form 1041- U.S. Income Tax Return for Estates and Trusts is required for the estate or trust INCOME after a person dies. There are thresholds below which you do <u>not</u> have to file a return.

For example, assume Jerry dies and he has a probate estate which is distributed to a trust for the benefit of Molly. While Jerry's estate is open, the estate will file an IRS Form 1041 for any estate income and expenses. When the trust receives funds and is administered, then the trustee will file an IRS Form 1041 for the trust income and expenses.

IRS Form 1041 can be extremely complicated to complete and it is important that you have a competent CPA or tax attorney to complete this IRS form.

Chapter 8: Retirement Benefits

Sara has three million dollars in her individual retirement account ("IRA") and approximately three million dollars in other assets including her homestead. She has charitable intent but also wants to provide for her children and various nieces and nephews. She is quite confused as to whom she should name as the beneficiary of her IRA. She has heard about Revocable Trusts and wants to create a Revocable Trust but does not understand whether she should change the beneficiary designation of her IRA to her Revocable Trust. She keeps hearing about the terms "see-through trust" and "conduit trust", but is very confused and cannot decide whether her Revocable Trust, her charities or her children, nieces and nephews should be the beneficiary of her IRA.

Questions:

1. What is the difference in how assets are distributed at death between a beneficiary designation of an IRA, assets in your own name or a Revocable Trust?

As discussed in Chapter 5 and Chapter 6, assets held in a decedent's name or Revocable Trust will be distributed to the beneficiaries either through a probate or a trust administration. However, because a decedent has typically signed beneficiary designations for assets held in an IRA, the IRA assets are distributed directly to the named beneficiaries pursuant to the beneficiary designations without becoming part of a probate or trust administration. If, however, the estate or the Revocable Trust is the named beneficiary, those distributions become assets of the estate or Revocable Trust and distributed according to the terms of the Last Will and Testament or the Revocable Trust. The IRA rules are extremely complicated and care must be given when making a beneficiary designation.

2. What is the advantage of naming an individual as a beneficiary of my IRA instead of my Revocable Trust?

The rules for distributions from IRAs and other retirement benefits are extremely complicated. The primary benefit of naming an individual is that individual can be a designated beneficiary ("DB") and a DB can (with few exceptions) take distributions from an IRA over their life expectancy while keeping the assets within the IRA to grow tax free until distributions are required.

If the estate or Revocable Trust is named as a beneficiary, the estate or Revocable Trust is not considered a DB and the payout is over a much shorter time frame unless special rules are followed.

3. Is there any way my Revocable Trust beneficiaries can receive favorable deferrals?

Yes, if the Revocable Trust is drafted properly.

4. What is an Accumulation Trust?

An Accumulation Trust is one in which the trustee accumulates income for a period of time set forth in the document before making distribution to the beneficiary(ies). This type of trust does <u>not</u> guaranty that the beneficiaries will receive the favorable deferral payout.

5. What is a Conduit Trust?

A conduit trust is a type of trust where the trustee has no power to accumulate plan distributions in the trust. The IRS considers the conduit trust beneficiary as the sole beneficiary, disregarding all other beneficiaries. A conduit trust requires the trustee to distribute to the beneficiary any distributions the conduit trust receives after the participant's death and during the beneficiary's lifetime.

6. What if I want to name a charity(ies) as beneficiary(ies) of my Trust? Is it better to name the charity as a direct beneficiary of my IRA?

If you do not have an IRA and want to name a charity as a beneficiary of your assets, you have several options available as shown in Chapter 8.   Tax benefits for the charities and your taxable estate differ with each option. However, if you have an IRA and name a charity as a direct beneficiary, not only will the charity <u>not</u> have to pay income taxes on your donation when it receives the IRA assets, the estate tax burden for your family would be decreased, as your estate would receive a charitable deduction on the IRA account's value.

7. Is it better to just forget a Revocable Trust and name individuals as beneficiaries of my IRA?

It depends. Because inherited IRAs allow for stretch-out tax benefits for named beneficiaries, you should consult with both your financial advisor and attorney in determining how to distribute your IRA to consider your family structure and allow for maximum transfer of the IRA funds. If you name an individual as a beneficiary, then the individual may take distributions over their life expectancy, but they can always take the full amount and pay income taxes. Thus, if you want to control the timing of the distributions, then the Revocable Trust may be the best alternative, assuming the Revocable Trust is drafted properly.

8. What about contingent beneficiaries? Should I have them?

It is crucial to name contingent beneficiaries for any accounts, including IRAs. If you have only a primary beneficiary and that beneficiary predeceases you, the distribution of your IRA account may be determined by the IRA custodian's default policy which could be an estate which has the least favorable tax consequences.

9. If my custodian or owner/company that operates my IRA is merged into another company, then will my beneficiary designation still work?

If the custodian of your IRA changes, your original beneficiary designation should remain in force. However, the new custodian may ask you to update your beneficiary designation(s) on their forms, and if they do not ask, you should follow-up to confirm they have the proper beneficiary designations.

10. Should I periodically review my beneficiary designations?

Yes! You should periodically review all your beneficiary designations to ensure that the persons or charities you have named as beneficiaries are still the ones that you wish to receive these accounts.

11. How can I make sure that the provider has the correct beneficiary designations?

You may contact the custodian/provider at any time and request a copy of the beneficiary designations they have on file for you.

12. Should I have a custom made beneficiary designation?

It is always a good idea to have your lawyer review your beneficiary designations. You want to be sure they are fully coordinated with other estate planning documents and do not defeat your intentions you have drafted in other documents but will work with what you have already drafted.

13. What if I have a retirement plan that is not an IRA, such as a 401(k) plan, with my employer?

Check <u>all</u> beneficiary designations (including contingent beneficiaries) and read the plan contract. If an individual dies while at the company, many 401(k) plans require a lump sum payout to the beneficiary which can result in drastic tax consequences. Fortunately, through the beneficiary of the inherited account should be able to roll it over into an inherited IRA.

Chapter 9: Alternative Estate Planning Techniques

Betty has three children, Amy, Bradley and Cooper and an estate of $500,000, which consists of her house and stocks and bonds. She has heard about a Last Will and Testament and a Revocable Trust, and frankly doesn't want to spend the money to pay for such documents or hire an attorney to prepare them. Does Betty have any alternatives, and if so, what are the risks?

Questions:

1. What types of ownership of property are allowed in Florida which may permit Betty to transfer her assets without hiring an attorney?

Assets such as real estate, bank accounts and stocks and bonds can be held jointly with right of survivorship ("JTWROS"), which means that upon one party's death the survivor receives such account. JTWROS could result in the dis-inheritance of other family members. If an account is titled "Betty JTWROS Amy", then Bradley and Cooper would be disinherited because nothing legally requires Amy to give any of those funds or real estate to Bradley or Cooper. Florida law requires that the title to real estate must specifically state: "joint tenants with right of survivorship". Otherwise, the ownership may be construed as tenants-in-common ("TIC").

Tenants-in-Common ("TIC") does not have the element of survivorship. Property owned in this manner will pass under each owner's Last Will and Testament (or via intestacy if there is no Last Will and

Testament) upon death. Florida law presumes TIC with non-spouses, if not clearly stated JTWROS property.

Tenancy-by-the-Entirety ("TBE") is joint ownership of property by a married couple and provides that the survivor will own the property upon the death of the other spouse. Neither spouse can sell, gift nor convey their undivided one-half interest without the joinder of the other spouse. In Florida, real property titled in the name of a married couple is presumed to be TBE property. However, it is a good idea to title any real property by spouses as follows: John Brown and Mary Brown, Husband and Wife, as tenants-by-the-entirety.

JTWROS Example: Sue and Betty (sisters) own a home as JTWROS. At Sue's death, Betty would own 100% of the home.

TIC Example: Sue and Betty (sisters) own a home as TIC. At Sue's death, Sue's Last Will and Testament, if any, of if no Last Will and Testament, Florida law, would direct whom would receive Sue's 50% share and Betty would own a 50% share.

TBE Example: Sue and Betty (a married couple) own a home as TBE. At Sue's death, Betty would own 100% of the home.

2. What are some of the dangers of Betty owning property jointly with Amy, Bradley or Cooper?

If Amy, Bradley or Cooper were involved in litigation which results in a judgment or if either owe taxes or either cause an automobile accident which results in a judgement, then the property will be subject to attachment by those creditors, even if that joint owner is on the title to only avoid probate.

If a child became incapacitated and the property is jointly-owned real estate, then a court appointed guardian may have to be obtained to sell the real estate.

If Betty only had Cooper on a title, then if Betty died first only Cooper would receive the property and Amy and Bradley would be disinherited.

If Betty names a child as a co-owner there could be gift tax, and there can be a great deal of tax uncertainty with respect to whether a gift is made when a joint account is set up and who should pay the income tax on interest earned by a joint account. Further, if a child is put on a real estate title and their share is more than the annual gift exclusion (currently $14,000) then a Form 709 – United States Gift Tax Return must be filed.

Finally, favorable homestead attributes can be lost. See Chapter 11 for more information regarding homestead.

3. Can a POD account help Betty's situation?

Certain assets can be titled in Betty's name with a POD beneficiary at her death. Betty would have use of the account during her lifetime, and upon her death, the account transfers directly to the individual(s) she designates. This avoids many of the problems associated with joint ownership and also avoids probate. A typical designation would read "Betty POD Amy." Of course, if Betty only names Amy, then Bradley and Cooper will receive nothing.

4. What happens if a POD beneficiary dies before Betty and Betty becomes incapacitated?

If the named beneficiary on the account dies before Betty and Betty becomes incapacitated before she can name a new POD beneficiary, then upon Betty's death, the assets will pass through probate. If Betty has a DPOA, then an agent can name a beneficiary (see Chapter 4) if the DPOA permits such power.

5. What if Betty owned life insurance or an IRA?

Betty could then name Amy, Bradley and Cooper as equal beneficiaries.

Chapter 10: The Surviving Spouse

Amanda and John are in their late fifties and have children from prior marriages. This is Amanda's second marriage and John's third marriage. Each has accumulated quite a bit of wealth separately and do not want to see their step-children inherit their wealth. They have not signed a prenuptial or postnuptial agreement. They have heard about the Florida elective share and other spousal rights, but do not understand those rights and do not want to pay two separate attorneys to prepare postnuptial documents defining their rights upon divorce and death. They are also very concerned that they don't want to "hurt each other's feelings" because it appears that they do not trust each other.

Questions:

1. What happens if Amanda dies and makes no provision for John because she does not want John to give her money to his children?

In Florida, if Amanda did not provide for John, then John has the right to "elect" an elective share amount (30% of Amanda's assets). For example, if Amanda's estate is $1,000,000, then John would be entitled to $300,000. If John did not otherwise receive that amount, either through Amanda's Last Will and Testament, Revocable Trust and/or beneficiary designations, then John can make an election to take the elective share. The $300,000 is then satisfied with assets distributed to John directly, including, but not limited to, life insurance, IRAs, pension plans and trust assets and any balance is paid to John from Amanda's assets. Further, John would also be treated as a pretermitted spouse and be entitled to 50% of the probate assets.

2. Who can make an elective share election?

A spouse married to the decedent at the time of the decedent's death can make the elective share election.

3. Is there a way to avoid the elective share election?

By executing a prenuptial (prior to marriage) or postnuptial agreement (after marriage), Amanda and John can waive the elective share right. Absent those agreements John would be entitled to 30%. If Amanda has already provided for John's 30% share, such as through a beneficiary designation, then John is not entitled to more assets. Note that John, as a surviving spouse, is also entitled to an interest in Amanda's homestead if the homestead is owned in Amanda's name. See Chapter 11 for more information regarding homestead.

4. Absent a waiver of spousal rights, is there a way Amanda can affirmatively plan for giving John assets in trust without giving him the assets outright?

Yes, Amanda can make provisions in her Last Will and Testament and a Revocable Trust that, if John makes an elective share election, then an Elective Share Trust ("EST") can be created.

The $300,000 previously discussed can be satisfied by utilizing an EST. If the EST provides only income to a spouse, then the EST is a 50% trust and must contain $600,000 (50% x $600,000 = $300,000) to provide the elective share amount. If the EST provides for income _and_ principal for health, support and maintenance, then the EST is an 80% trust and

must contain $375,000 (80% x $375,000 = $300,000) to provide the elective share amount.

5. What other spousal rights does John have if he does not waive such rights?

Absent a waiver of rights, in addition to the elective share election, spousal rights include an intestate share (if there is no Last Will and Testament), pretermitted share, homestead, exempt property, family allowance, and preference in appointment as personal representative of an intestate estate.

6. Is there a risk of Amanda creating trusts for her children with John being the trustee and managing the assets while he is still living?

Any time you have a surviving spouse managing money for step-children, there is ample opportunity for strife and discord. Further, if John is also entitled to income or principal from the trust, his interest will directly conflict with the step-children's interests. What if John uses all of the trust funds? Trust accountings are required to be sent to the step-children. If they do not agree with the accounting then objections can be filed and litigation could ensue.

7. What affect does this marriage have on portability (previously discussed in Chapter 7)?

When Amanda dies, if she has not used all of her unused applicable exclusion amount ($5.490 million in 2017), John can file an estate tax return to "port" over Amanda's unused exclusion amount for his benefit. This portability may possibly save estate taxes for the benefit of John's children. Thus, an issue will arise as to who should pay the expenses for preparing and filing the estate tax return if portability is elected.

8. Should Amanda's children pay for this portability benefit of $2.196 million ($5.490 million times 40%) which will benefit John's children?

Amanda probably would not want this result so this responsibility should be made clear in the estate planning documents and/or prenuptial or postnuptial agreement.

Chapter 11: Homestead

Amanda and John, a married couple, have heard about the Florida laws on homestead but don't really understand how homestead applies to them. They assume that because they own their homestead as TBE (see discussion in Chapter 9 and Chapter 10), and, as discussed in Chapter 10, they know that when one of them dies, the homestead will be automatically distributed to the surviving spouse. What happens, however, upon the surviving spouse's death?

Questions:

1. What is homestead in the state of Florida?

Under the Florida Constitution, a person's homestead is entitled to certain protection. The homestead must meet certain requirements: if located within a municipality, to the extent of one-half acre of contiguous land, or if located outside a municipality, to the extent of one hundred sixty acres of contiguous land and improvements thereon. A person's homestead is not subject to claims of creditors (other than creditors who have worked on the homestead or a mortgage secured by the homestead). Thus, a creditor cannot force one to sell one's home to pay off one's debts. This applies even if a person has filed bankruptcy, assuming that a person has lived in Florida the requisite amount of time. A person's homestead is also eligible for a $50,000 annual exemption against the assessed value for purposes of calculating the ad valorem taxes on the property and the favorable "save our home cap" which limits annual increases in real estate taxes. The Florida

Constitution also provides limitation on the descent and devise of homestead.

2. Assume the homestead is only in Amanda's name. Can Amanda devise the homestead only to her children?

If Amanda dies and leaves no minor children, then the homestead may <u>only</u> be devised outright in fee simple to John. If the property is not devised outright to John, and Amanda is survived by <u>any</u> children, then John will receive a life estate and Amanda's lineal descendants will receive the remainder. Florida now provides that John can elect to hold the homestead as TIC (see discussion in Chapter 9) with Amanda's children instead of a life estate.

3. Is there a way to avoid the Constitutional restrictions on the descent and devise of the homestead?

Under Florida law, there are restrictions on how a person's homestead may be devised at death. If there are minor children or a surviving spouse, Florida law requires the homestead be devised in a certain manner. Of course, a spouse can always waive their rights in the homestead via a prenuptial or postnuptial agreement.

If, however, Amanda and John own the homestead as TBE regardless of whether or not there are minor children, then the homestead will be distributed to John upon Amanda's death.

If Amanda owns a homestead and is not survived by John or minor children, then she can devise the homestead to whomever she designates in her Last Will and Testament or Revocable Trust.

4. What if Amanda and John have a minor child?

If either Amanda or John were to die, leaving one or more minor children, then, if the homestead is titled in only John or Amanda's name, the surviving spouse would take a life estate in the property and the minor child(ren) would retain the remainder interest. Florida law also provides that, in such a case, the spouse can elect to take a 50% tenant in common interest. If the homestead is titled in both John and Amanda's names, then they own the homestead as TBE and the homestead devise restrictions do not apply and upon either John or Amanda's death, the homestead would be distributed to the surviving spouse.

5. Amanda and John own the homestead as TBE. Upon the survivor's death, the survivor devises the homestead to all their adult children (they have no minor children). Are there advantages to this devise or should the surviving spouse's personal representative sell the homestead and distribute the proceeds equally between all of the children?

If the homestead is devised directly to the children, then the children will receive the homestead free of the <u>surviving spouse's</u> creditors. After the homestead is distributed to their children, then they can sell the homestead.

Alternatively, if the personal representative sells the homestead and distributes the proceeds to the children, all of the proceeds are subject to the <u>surviving spouse's</u> creditors.

6. If Amanda and John own the homestead and have a minor child from their marriage and both Amanda and John have adult children from their prior marriages, then does the homestead have to be devised to the minor child upon the latter of Amanda or John's death?

Not exclusively but, upon the death of the surviving spouse, if they have a minor child, then the homestead <u>must</u> be distributed to all the children with the minor child's share held in a guardianship.

7. Is there absolutely no way around the devise restriction upon a homestead?

Section 732.4017 of the Florida Statute was enacted to provide for a special type of trust to possibly avoid homestead restrictions. This trust must be drafted very carefully and it has not yet been tested in the Florida courts. PROCEED WITH CAUTION!

Chapter 12: Basic Asset Protection

After a long stressful day at work, Tom finally leaves the office to head home. On his way home, Tom accidently hits a person on a bicycle. The cyclist does not die, but incurs severe head injuries and other medical problems. While Tom is the owner of the car and an insured driver, he and his wife, Jane, are worried about a lawsuit. Tom and Jane currently have assets that consist of a homestead (owned as TBE), a banking and savings account titled in joint names, a stock account titled in Tom's name, a bank account titled in Jane's name, an IRA for each of them, and two vehicles, each titled in their own name. Tom and Jane seek an attorney to review their estate plan and asset protection options.

Questions:

1. What assets, if any, are susceptible to a lawsuit?

Under Florida law, Tom's homestead, retirement accounts, annuities and assets held as TBE are not subject to the claims of Tom's creditors.

2. How should Tom and Jane's assets be titled?

As described in Chapter 9, assets held as TBE is the most protection afforded to *married* Florida residents. Assets titled as TBE are generally not subject to the claims of creditors of one spouse. This protection is not afforded to assets titled as JTWROS or TIC (see Chapter 9 for definition of terms).

3. How do jointly titled assets affect the estate plan?

It is very important to carefully consider how to title one's assets. If a married couple has bank accounts titled in separate names or in their separate revocable trust, then retitling should be reviewed to determine whether assets should be titled as TBE.

Furthermore, if Tom and Jane have a joint trust, or separate trusts, Tom and Jane need to decide if titling assets in the name of the trust outweighs the benefit of avoiding probate or asset protection.

Another issue is if Tom and Jane have children from a previous marriage. It is quite common for spouses to keep assets separated to devise certain assets to their children from a prior marriage. Again, Tom and Jane will need to decide if the titling of assets in separate names or a Revocable Trust outweigh the benefits of TBE.

Many scenarios need to be considered when deciding to title assets as TBE, separately or in the name of a trust. These difficult decisions should be discussed with an experienced estate planning attorney who can assist you in weighing all of the options to determine what works best for you and your family.

4. Are TBE assets subject to probate?

It is important to remember that TBE assets automatically pass to the surviving spouse and (typically) do not involve the probate process until the survivor's death.

5. What is an umbrella policy?

An umbrella policy is an insurance policy that provides liability coverage over and above your automobile or homeowner's policy. Thus, if Tom's automobile insurance is not sufficient to cover the damages of the accident, an umbrella policy may help bridge the gap and possibly avoid having a lien on Tom's assets.

6. How should Tom and Jane's vehicles be titled?

Each person's vehicle should be titled in his or her own name alone. Thus, if Tom's vehicle is titled in his name alone, his jointly held assets cannot be subject to a claim. Only assets titled in Tom's name alone will be subject to a claim. Conversely, if Tom and Jane's vehicles are titled in joint names, then all of their TBE assets can be subject to claims of creditors.

This principle should also be applied to other forms of vehicles such as ATVs, boats and jet skis.

7. What if Tom and Jane's 17 year old son, Jeff, caused the accident?

Another important conversation to have with your estate planning attorney is considering how to title assets when children are involved. As with most parents, they want to help their children and buy them cars for graduation or a birthday present. Or, as with most minors, they do not have sufficient credit to purchase a vehicle and the parents want to help their child.

Most often, the parents will title the name of the vehicle in their name and allow their child to drive the vehicle. There is no need to discuss how easy it can be for a young, inexperienced driver to make a mistake on the road. However, it is important to discuss with your estate planning attorney how that "mistake" will affect you financially. It is the best practice to title the vehicle in the child's name alone, even if it causes higher insurance premiums. Again, it must be determined if higher insurance premiums outweigh the possibility of a lawsuit or credit claims on individually owned assets of the parent who is named on the car. It is also important to note that there is Florida case law that has attached "co-owners" of a vehicle even if the co-owner never intended to drive the vehicle.

8. Are there any other legal answers for protection from liability?

Yes, you can be afforded asset protection through corporations, limited liability companies, partnerships and various trusts. States other than Florida may also offer more protections, depending on your needs. These types of questions need to be discussed with your attorney.

Chapter 13: Medicare and Medicaid Planning

Many of us confuse Medicare and Medicaid. These questions and answers will explain the differences and how death affects benefits.

Questions:

1. What is the difference between Medicare and Medicaid?

Medicare is a federal health insurance program. Medicare falls short of providing long term care, such as nursing home or other long term care benefits.

Medicaid is a federally-funded, state-administered program which provides such benefits as nursing home care to individuals who qualify.

2. Upon my parent's death, do I need to worry about Medicare or Medicaid?

As to Medicare, no, except to be sure that health insurance benefits have been or will be paid. If a hospital or doctor has not been paid they may file a claim to the estate. Many times the claim is filed prior to receipt of Medicare payment. Before satisfying the claim, be sure Medicare has paid as much as required.

As to Medicaid, if a probate is opened, then a notice to creditors, together with the decedent's death certificate must be sent to the Agency of Health Administration (the agency administering Medicaid), if the individual is over the age of 55. If the decedent was on Medicaid, then a notice to creditor should be sent, regardless of age.

3. What are issues if I distribute money and I know nothing about Medicaid?

In some cases, beneficiaries may not know whether the decedent received Medicaid benefits. In such cases, it is always a good idea to send the notice to creditors to the agency prior to distribution of the assets.

4. If I want to plan for Medicaid, who do I contact?

You should contact an attorney who is board certified in Elder law. You can find these attorneys on www.flabar.org or contact our office for a referral.

Chapter 14: Choosing a Competent Attorney

Now that you have read this book and see many issues as to planning, drafting and implementing an estate plan, how do you go about hiring a competent estate planning attorney?

1. Referrals. Ask your friends, CPAs, financial advisors, etc. if they have an estate planning attorney they trust.

2. Board Certification. When reading an attorney's biography, look for the designation "Florida Board Certified Attorney in Wills, Trusts and Estates." These attorneys must have practiced in these areas for at least five (5) years, take a grueling exam and have recommendations from their peers as to the attorney's ethics, expertise and quality of work. Board certification designation should not be confused with adjectives like "expertise" or "specialist" but look for the specific "Florida Board Certified" language.

3. Website Information. Take the time to research the attorney. Read their biography and other information on the attorney's website. Look to see if the attorney regularly attends continuing education, gives lectures, writes articles, etc.

4. Florida Bar Website. Review the Florida Bar website to review any ethical violations an attorney may have. The Florida Bar's website is easy to use and has a directory to assist in locating information for a Florida attorney.

5. Real Property, Probate and Trust Law Attorneys. Look for attorneys that are <u>active</u> members in the Florida Bar's Real Property, Probate and Trust Law Section.

6. American College of Trust and Estate Planning. Look for attorneys that are members of the American College of Trust and Estate Planning, a national organization of lawyers elected to membership by demonstrating the highest level of integrity, commitment to the profession, competence and experience as trust and estate counselors.

7. Quality v. Quantity. Do not just focus on price. As the old saying goes "You get what you pay for", just remember, quality work and peace of mind is priceless.

Made in the USA
Columbia, SC
10 February 2025

52969574R00040